The Life of an Architect...

...AND WHAT HE
LEAVES BEHIND...

A
DOM
publishers

arch.

The Characters

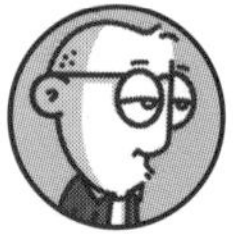

ARCHIBALD,
THE ARCHITECT

Always dressed in a black suit, Archibald is a romantic architect, a dreamer who takes architecture very seriously. He runs an architecture office with his partner and engineer, Gerald. While Archibald is a visionary and a romantic dreamer with a tendency to idealistic and egocentric behavior, Gerald is the rational one. In their office also work, among many others, an exploited intern named Ralph, a narrow-minded IT-specialist named John, and a weird Asian cardboard model builder named Mr. Shan. On the whole, Archibald's a man with a vision, but mostly a vision that the others don't share. He holds on to old values such as paper and pencil and his drawing board. One thing is certain: his view on life makes you think about it, whether your response is a smile or a grin...

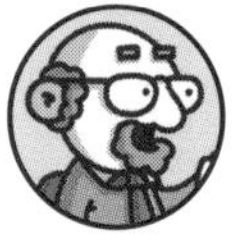

GERALD,
THE ENGINEER

Gerald is an engineering graduate, associate, colleague, neighbor and a faithful friend of Archibald. Unlike Archibald, Gerald is a rational man. His primary task is to keep Archibald with both his feet on the ground by asking probing questions at regular intervals.

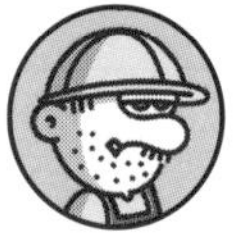

FRED,
THE CONTRACTOR

Fred is the man who has to put Archibald's ideas into practice. He's a very practical man with a dry sense of humor and hates architects who propose ideas that are impossible to carry out. No wonder that he often clashes with Archibald.

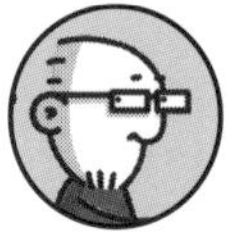

RALPH,
THE INTERN

The inexperienced but super-motivated and freshly graduated intern faces the harsh reality of the building world in Archibald's office. Exploitation by Archibald and a distinct generation gap between him and his internship supervisor cause inevitable tensions.

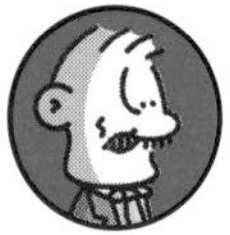

FRANK,
THE PROJECT DEVELOPER

Frank has no interest at all in architecture. The only reason he develops projects is because of the money. Because he hasn't enough work and he has a family to support, Archibald is compelled to execute the wishes of this developing devil against his best wishes.

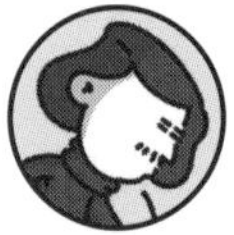

MR. SHAN,
THE MODEL BUILDER

Indisputably the world's best model builder. Specialized in cardboard, he reproduces anything to any scale, which is no mean feat. Mr. Shan uses his precision knife as if it were a musketeer's sword, while his Oriental looks indicate a former career as origami artist.

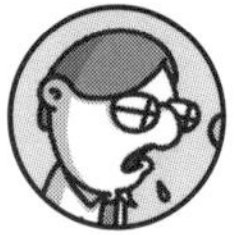

JOHN,
THE CAD MANAGER

Within Archibald's office, the software architect is a computer expert who is responsible for all the hard- and software. You can imagine how hard his job is if you know that Archibald hates computers. The software architect is a real specialist, a genuine computer nerd that every firm needs.

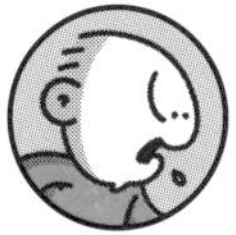

JULIUS,
THE CLIENT

To Archibald, clients are a necessary evil; he'd much prefer building without them. For Julius, everything is too expensive. He keeps asking for adaptations and cannot grasp Archibald's theories. To him, all houses are the same and that's how he wants to keep it.

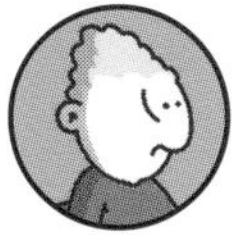

MARIA,
THE CLIENT'S WIFE

Shares the popular roots of her husband, but, although hard to believe, she's even worse. She only says superfluous things that have nothing to do with the subject at hand, thus rendering herself a nuisance. A client is bad, but a client's spouse is even worse.

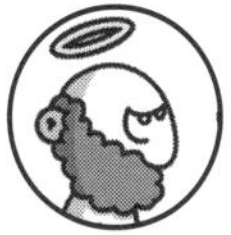

GOD,
HIMSELF

God is the supreme architect. He created the world in seven days, but not always according to Archibald's architectural insights. Archibald regularly goes to see God, complaining about the world He created. Archibald's mission in life is therefore to redo and improve God's work.

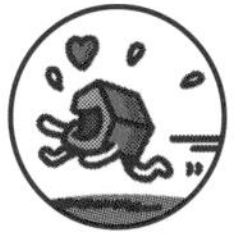

THE CONCEPT,
THE MODEL

The model embodies Archibald's architectural concepts and innovative ideas. Strong-minded, strong-willed and opinionated, the model really wants to take part in this architectural quest during which it not only repeatedly questions itself, but also Archibald.

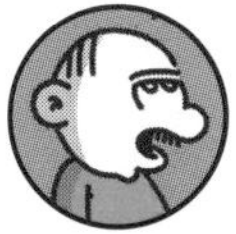

GEORGE,
THE BUREAUCRAT

George is slow and therefore outstanding in impeding the process. He is also illogical, since he doesn't know a thing about architecture (he was transferred from another administration) but pretends to know everything better. In short, he is the typical municipal urban planning officer.

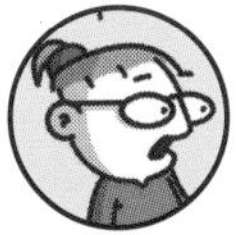

CHARLOTTE,
ARCHIBALD'S WIFE

Charlotte is married to Archibald. She's a practicing attorney at the bar. To the great annoyance of Archibald she is very rational and always refutes his theories on architecture. She is a woman who lives by the small print. No detail, architectural or not, will escape her attention.

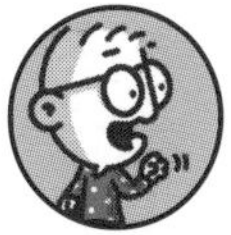

ARCHIE,
ARCHIBALD'S SON

Archie wants to be everything his father is, but ten times better. Fiercely intelligent, he always has a quick retort when asked a question. Ever since he was born, he has been obsessed with architecture and has but one goal in life: to become the world's best architect.

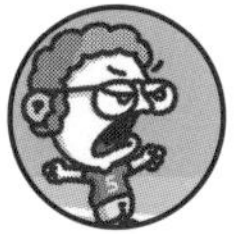

GERRY,
GERALD'S SON

Although he doesn't always understand him, Gerry is Archie's best friend. The two of them made a secret pact in which they decided they're both going to make it in the construction world. Therefore, it is safe to say that the two best friends are not short of ambition.

WHAT DO YOU SEE?
A HOUSE...
NOW LOOK AT MY FEE AND THEN TAKE ANOTHER LOOK...
WHAT DO YOU SEE NOW?
A WORK OF ART...

THIS IS NOT THE ACOUSTIC INSULATION ACCORDING TO SPECIFICATIONS !
HEY ! WHOA ! DON'T YOU HEAR ME ?!
THIS TYPE IS MUCH BETTER...IT ABSORBS ALL SURROUNDING SOUNDS BEFORE IT HAS BEEN PLACED...

AND THÁT YOU WANT TO SEPARATE ?

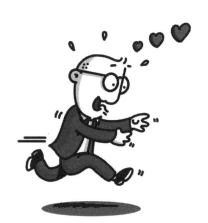

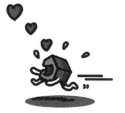

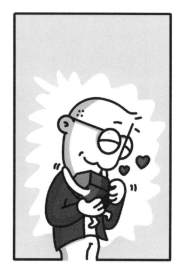

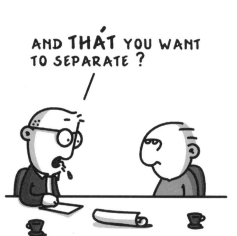

THE RENOVATION OF THE BANKRUPTCY AGENCY WAS A REAL CHALLENGE...
ESPECIALLY THE LIGHTS IN THE WAITING ROOM...

GOD, THE WORLD IS IN TROUBLE... WHAT ARE YOU GOING TO DO ABOUT IT?
WHAT DID HE SAY?
HE DOESN'T DO CONSTRUCTION SITE SUPERVISION...

I DON'T HAVE A PROBLEM THAT HE'S DRAWING ON THE WALLS DURING CONSTRUCTION...
BUT THE FRAMES ARE TOO MUCH...

SHALL I TELL YOU A JOKE BEFORE WE START THE MEETING?
IS IT A GOOD ONE?
SURE...
OK... SHOW ME YOUR DESIGN...

WHY DO YOU ABSOLUTELY WANT TO PLACE A SINGLE BRICK IN A SEPARATE LOCKED LAYER?
HEHE

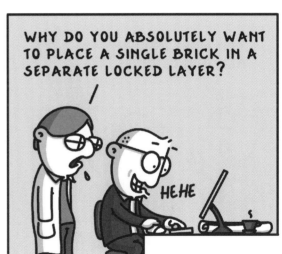

YOU MUST ROLL IN ALL DIRECTIONS...
EXCEPT IN MY DIRECTION...

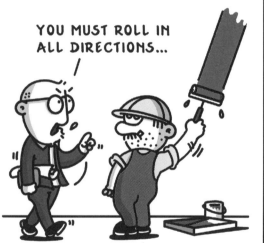

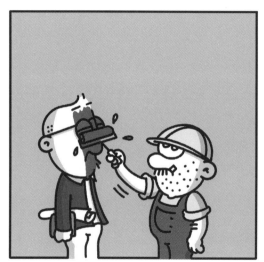

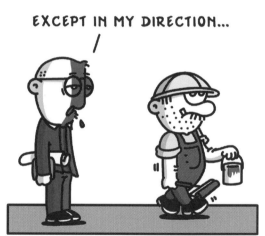

THIS BUILDING IS DESIGNED IN A WAY THAT, WHEN YOU WALK AROUND IT IN THE CITY, YOU SEE A DIFFERENT BUILDING EVERY TIME...IT HAS MANY IDENTITIES...
WHEN I SPIN AROUND, DOES IT MAKE ME A DIFFERENT PERSON?
ENGINEERS TAKE ALL THE FUN OUT OF DESIGNING...

DAD, ANOTHER HUNDRED OR SO HOUSES ARE WASHED AWAY AGAIN BY A TSUNAMI...
SOMETIMES GOD HAS OTHER PLANS WITH SOME AREAS...
HOW?
THIS COULD HAVE BEEN AVOIDED...
BY ASKING GOD THE BUILDING REGULATIONS BEFOREHAND...

DAD, COULD YOU CHECK MY EYE? I THINK THERE'S SOMETHING IN IT...
I THINK IT'S A DOOR...
A DOOR?
YEAH, EVERYTIME I CLOSE MY EYES I'M IN ANOTHER ROOM...

DAD, WHEN WILL I BE AN ACCOMPLISHED ARCHITECT?
ARCHITECTURE IS NOT A FINAL DESTINATION IN TIME... IT'S A JOURNEY THROUGH LIFE...
GREAT ! I LOVE TRAVELING !
WHERE CAN I BUY THE TICKETS?

SO...YOU WENT TO SCHOOL FOR 25 YEARS AND THEN YOU'RE WORKING FOR 30 YEARS TO PAY OFF THIS GIGANTIC AMOUNT OF MONEY THAT I CAN SQUANDER IN A FEW LINE?
IT'S MY DUTY TO ASSESS THEIR MOTIVATION...

LOOK ! THIS IS THE CITY YOU'RE GONNA BE PART OF...
OHH... HOW CUTE !
WHEEE
WHAT'S WRONG?
HE TAKES YOU FOR AN UGLY FAÇADE...
WHAAA

ZAP!!
ZAP!
WOW!
WHAT A DESIGN!

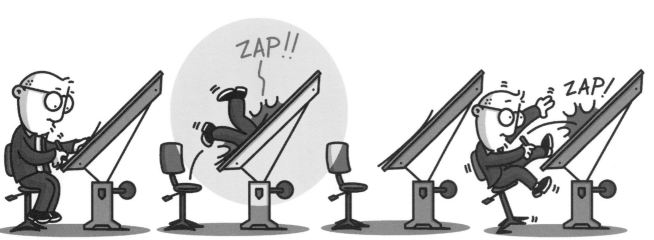

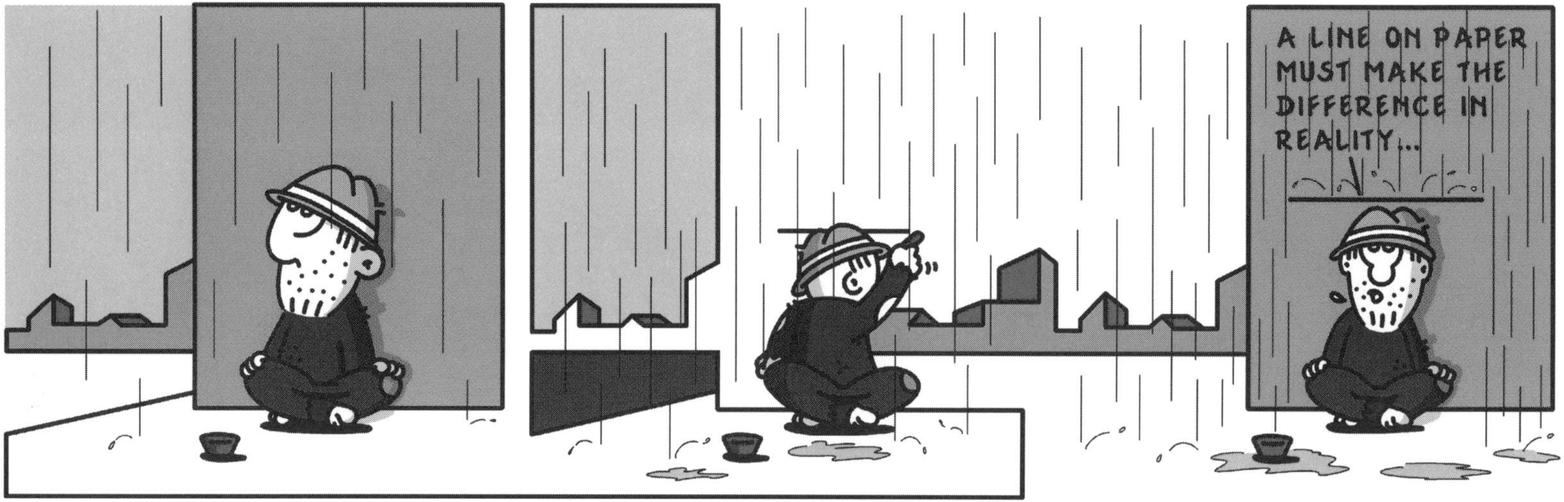
A LINE ON PAPER
MUST MAKE THE
DIFFERENCE IN
REALITY...

HOW COME ARCHITECTS ALWAYS ASK FOR IMPOSSIBLE THINGS?
MAYBE WE ARE LOUSY CONTRACTORS?
NAAAA!

LISTEN ARCHIE, I'VE HEARD YOU TALKING TO YOUR FRIEND... YOU CAN'T WORK FOR FREE...
WHY NOT? ARCHITECTURE IS FUN ISN'T IT?
BECOMING AN ARCHITECT TAKES YEARS OF HARD WORK... IT'S AN INVESTMENT THAT SHOULD PAY ITSELF BACK AS SOON AS POSSIBLE...
WELL DAD, THEN YOU'RE SURE GIVING ALL THE WRONG SIGNALS...
ALL THOSE FREE DESIGNS I'VE MADE FOR YOU THE PAST YEARS ARE SURELY NOT IN PROPORTION TO THE POCKET MONEY YOU'RE GIVING ME...

THE CLIENT IS HERE TO DISCUSS HIS REMARKS ON THE DESIGN...
I'VE SENT AN INTERN TO THE MEETING...
WHY?
FOR DANGEROUS STUNTS I USE A DOUBLE...

WHEN ARE YOU GOING TO APPROVE THE DESIGN?
DO YOU KNOW HOW DANGEROUS IT IS FOR A BUILDING TO BE IN THE TWILIGHT ZONE?
YOU KEEP IT LOCKED BETWEEN TWO WORLDS: THE WORLD OF IDEAS AND THE PHYSICAL WORLD...
IF IT CAN'T GET INTO IT'S BODY ANYMORE IT WILL BE YOUR FAULT...
WORKS EVERY TIME WITH CLIENTS WHO PRACTICE YOGA...
SHOW ME MY BODY !

HERE IS MY LAST WILL... GUARD IT WELL...
WHEN I DIE, I LIVE ON IN ALL MY BUILDINGS...
IS THIS CUSTOMARY WITH EVERY ARCHITECT?
NO... WHY DO YOU THINK THERE ARE SO MANY BUILDINGS WITHOUT A SOUL?
BADLY DRAWN UP WILL?

FALL ! FINALLY !
NOW I CAN FINALLY SEE...
THE BUILDINGS ACROSS THE STREET AGAIN...

DAD, WHEN DOES AN ARCHITECT TAKE VACATION?
NEVER... WE ARE ALWAYS BUSY WITH OUR DESIGNS...
WHAT DO YOU HAVE THERE?
A DESIGN FOR A VACATION AND NOW I'M OFF TO THE SITE...
BYE !

MY PLANS HAVE THE IMPACT OF A BOMB...

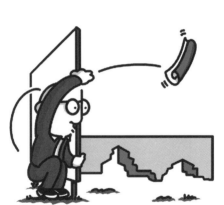

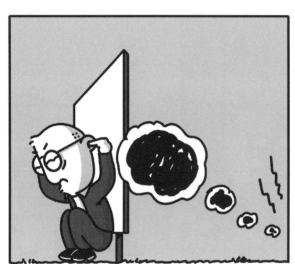

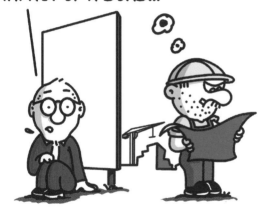

DON'T NAIL IT DOWN YET... THE ARCHITECT STILL HAS TO APPROVE THE PLANKS... I HAD TO REPLACE THEM BECAUSE HE SAID THEY WERE TOO THIN...
WACK
MASSIVE ENOUGH?

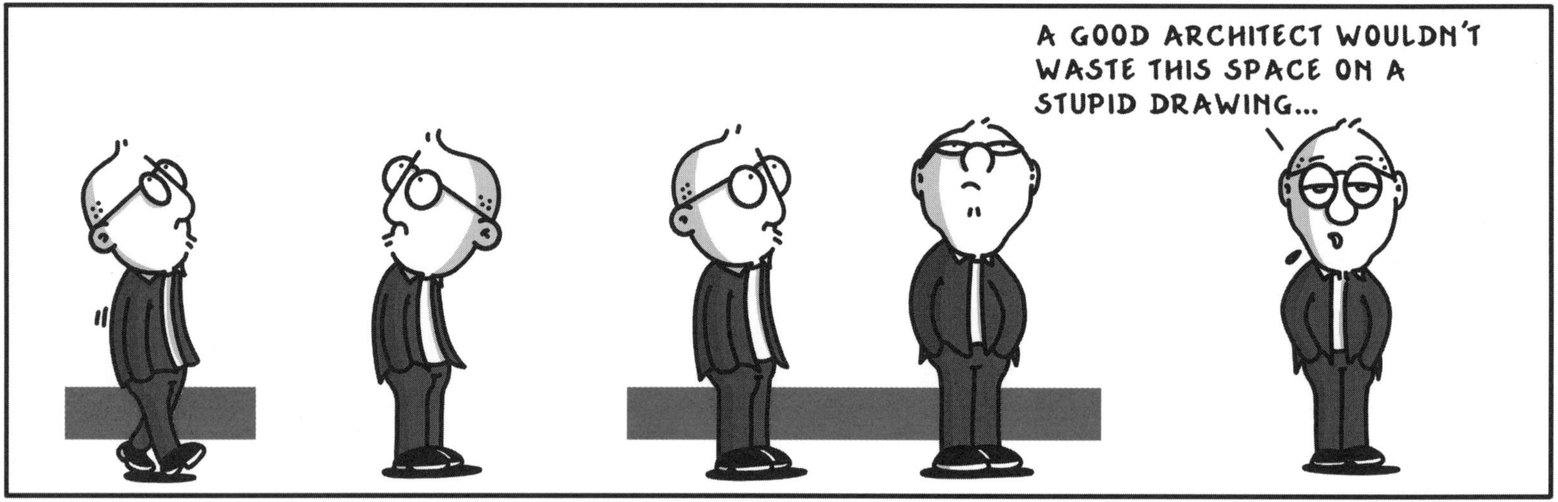
A GOOD ARCHITECT WOULDN'T WASTE THIS SPACE ON A STUPID DRAWING...

YOU MUST PLACE THIS LINE HERE...
I HAVE THE FEELING IT'S TIME TO SHOW MY DESIGN TO SOMEONE ELSE...

IN FRONT OF THE MIRROR AGAIN?
IS EVERYTHING OK?
AS LONG AS I SEE AN ARCHITECT BEFORE I SEE MYSELF, EVERYTHING IS OK...

YOU NEED TO ADD MORE WATER...
I NEVER SHOULD'VE TOLD HIM THAT HUMANS CONSIST OF 70% WATER...

THERE ARE TWO WORLDS: THE ONE I LIVE IN AND THE ONE IN MY THOUGHTS WHERE I CREATE AND I CONSTANTLY JUMP FROM ONE INTO THE OTHER...
I'M TRYING TO JOIN THEM, BUT THIS SELDOM WORKS...
WHO ARE YOU TALKING TO?
SORRY, WRONG WORLD...

FAREWELL... YOU'LL FIND YOUR WAY...
WHAT'S THAT AT THE END OF YOUR PENCIL?
WHEN I'M SKETCHING MY PENCIL IS ROAMING THE PAPER...

THERE'S AN ITEM IN THE SPECS FOR TEARING DOWN A THIRTY-FOOT HIGH WALL THAT ISN'T ON THE PLANS...
THAT'S THE WALL YOU'VE BUILT BETWEEN US...
THIS IS MY FEE FOR DRAWING UP THE DEMOLITION PERMIT... LUCKILY I'VE BEEN ABLE TO AVOID THE FINE FOR BUILDING AN ILLEGAL CONSTRUCTION...
EHH... THANKS I GUESS...
AND THEY SAY ARCHITECTS DON'T CARE ABOUT THEIR CLIENTS...

SLOF
SLOF
SLOF
SLOF
YOU HAVE
YOUR DESIGNS
ON YOU FEET...
THAT'S WHERE I WANT
MY CLIENTS TO BE...
SLOF
SLOF

CAN'T YOU MAKE THE ROOF THICKER?
NO, THAT WOULDN'T LOOK GOOD...
I DO THINK IT WOULD BE BETTER...
LET ME PUT IT DIFFERENTLY...

SIGHHH... I USED TO LOVE MY BODY...
WHAT HAPPENED?
I STARTED TO LOVE BUILDINGS INSTEAD...
MAYBE YOU SHOULD'VE STARTED WITH ORGANIC ARCHITECTURE...

WHERE DO I HAVE TO CONNECT THAT SEWER-PIPE TO?
THAT'S NOT A SEWER-PIPE
THAT PIPE WAS DESIGNED JUST IN CASE THE CLIENT WANTED A ROUND HOUSE...
I'LL SHOW YOU THE MODEL...
WHY DO I EVEN BOTHER ASKING THESE THINGS ?

ZAP
ZAP
ZAP
I'M GOING TO BED...
WHY?
ZAP
ZAP
THERE'S NOT A SINGLE DECENT BUILDING ON TV...

I'VE MADE IT EASY FOR YOU AND UPLOADED THE SPECS IN AUDIO ON AN I-POD...
THE NEXT DAY
WHAT HAPPENED HERE?!
I'VE USED THE SHUFFLE...

STOP THINKING LIKE AN ENGINEER !

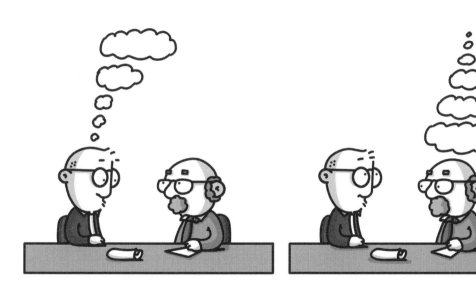

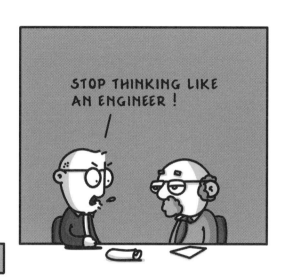

DO YOU HAVE MORE WORK FOR ME?
THE SPECS STATE THAT YOU HAVE TO LOVE MY DESIGN IN ORDER TO EXECUTE IT...
SO...DO YOU LOVE IT?
HOW CAN ANYONE LOVE ANYTHING WITH 200 PAGES OF FOREPLAY?

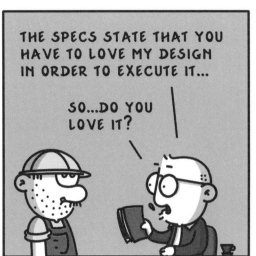

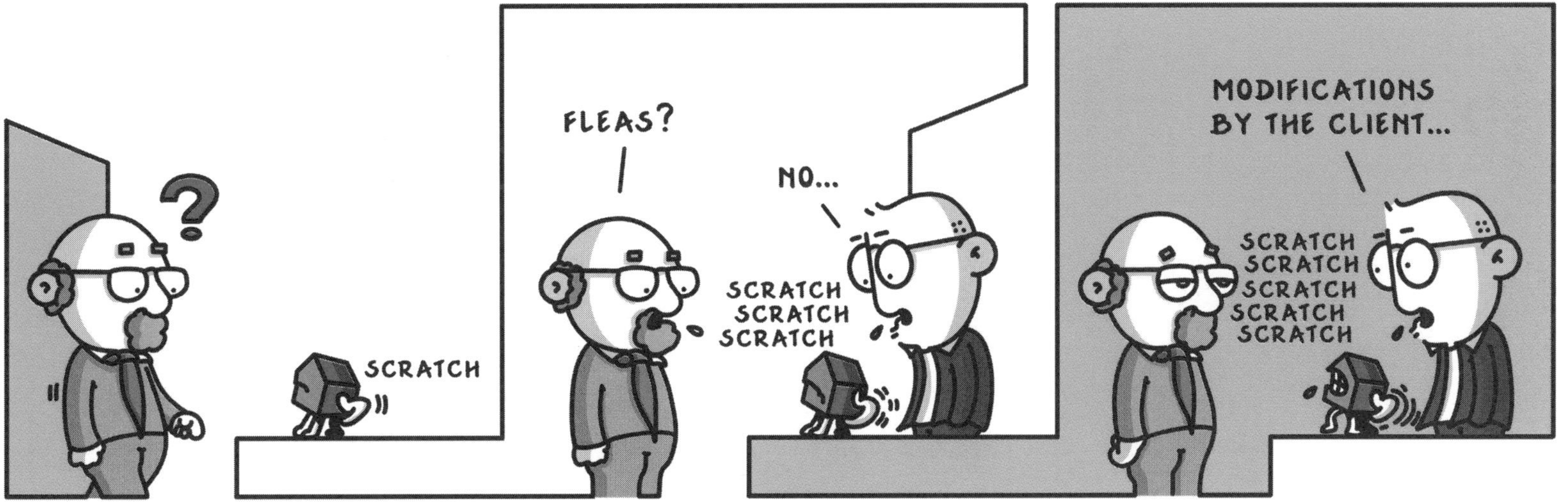
SCRATCH
FLEAS?
SCRATCH
SCRATCH
SCRATCH
NO...
MODIFICATIONS BY THE CLIENT...
SCRATCH
SCRATCH
SCRATCH
SCRATCH
SCRATCH

THE FIRST SNOW...
SOON THE WHOLE WORLD WILL BE COVERED WITH A WHITE CARPET...
NOBODY USES CARPET ANYMORE...

WHAT'S WRONG?

I CAN'T SEE ANYTHING...
THE WINDOW IS FOGGY...

NOW I CAN SEE...

THIS ONE?
NO !
AND THIS?
NO !
THIS?
NO !
I DON'T UNDERSTAND WHY YOU'RE UPSET... I'VE PUT ON A BOW TIE INSTEAD OF A REGULAR NECKTIE JUST LIKE YOU ASKED...

SPLAT

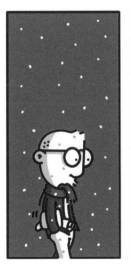

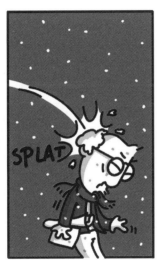

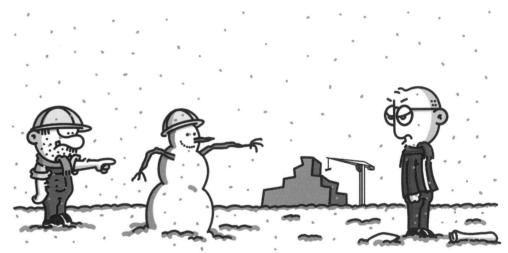

THERE ! DID YOU SEE THAT BUILDING?
NO I WAS WATCHING THE ACTOR...
YES, THAT'S WHAT I MEAN...
BUILDINGS DON'T ACT... THEY'RE ONLY DECORATION...
AND THEN I GAVE HER A LECTURE ABOUT ARCHITECTURE POSTURE...
PEOPLE DON'T KNOW HOW MANY YEARS OF PRACTICING IT TAKES TO PLAY MINIMALISM

YOU'RE STANDING IN...
WAIT ! I HAVE TO TAKE THIS CALL...
you are
standing in
concrete that
is drying
faster than I
can write
bye!

A CITY SHOULD BE LIKE A HUMAN BODY: IT SHOULD BE ABLE TO GROW AND BREAK DOWN ONE CELL AT A TIME...
YOU MEAN AT THE LEVEL OF A BRICK?
WACK!
A BRICK CONTAINS A WHOLE CITY OF CONTRACTORS...

NOWADAYS THERE'S A LOT OF SNOBBISHNESS WHEN IT COMES TO LIVING...
AND IT OCCURS IN ALL LEVELS OF THE POPULATION...
SEE WHAT I MEAN?

DAD, WHAT'S IT LIKE TO BE AN ARCHITECT?
I'M ALWAYS FIGHTING WITH CLIENTS AND CONTRACTORS TO KEEP THEM FROM INVADING MY DESIGNS...
I'M GONNA BE A DESIGN BOUNCER !

DO YOU KNOW WHAT ARCHITECTURE IS?
A BUILDING WITH MEGALOMANIA...
SELF-KNOWLEDGE IS THE BEGINNING OF ALL ARCHITECTURE...

I HAVE A BAD TASTE IN MY MOUTH...
I'VE PRONOUNCED THE AESTHETIC DEMANDS OF A CLIENT...
LET ME SMELL...
THAT MAKES EVERY ARCHITECT FALL OVER...
BAF

WHAT IS WITH YOU AND ROLLED-UP PLANS?
AND WHY ARE YOU CARRYING TWO SETS OF THE SAME DESIGN?
TRY THIS WITH FOLDED PLANS...
SLAP SLAP

I WANT A FEW EXTRA DORMER WINDOWS...
I'LL GET OUR ADJUSTMENTS ENGINEER...
IF YOU MAKE ONE MORE CHANGE YOUR HOUSE WILL DEFINITELY FALL TO PIECES...
I HATE THIS...
THE STABILITY OF MY IDEA IS IMPORTANT...

I'VE BEEN CALLING YOU ALL WEEK BUT YOU DON'T ANSWER YOUR PHONE !
I'VE BEEN WORKING ON THE BUILDING INSTEAD OF WORKING ON YOU...
BUT I AM THE CLIENT !
AND I AM A SUSTAINABLE ARCHITECT...
WHAT'S THAT GOT TO DO WITH IT?!
BUILDINGS LAST LONGER THAN CLIENTS...

WE NEED TO REDUCE THE DESIGN EXPENSES...
WE CAN CUT DOWN ON THE HOURS YOU MAKE ME LISTEN TO YOUR STUPID DESIGN REMARKS...
BY THE LOOK ON YOUR FACE I CAN TELL WE CAN SAVE SOME REAL MONEY THERE...

ARCHIBALD READS THE FUTURE OF YOUR DESIGNS
I DON'T SEE A SINGLE CHANGE IN YOUR LIFE...
BUT I WANT TO CHANGE A LOT OF THINGS !
PARALLEL FUTURES COST EXTRA...

HOW WIDE IS THE CORRIDOR?
I DON'T ALLOW CORRIDORS IN MY BUILDINGS...
WHY NOT?
A CORRIDOR IS A SUPERHIGHWAY BETWEEN ROOMS...
MY "PROMENADE ARCHITECTURALE" ONLY PERMITS A MAXIMUM SPEED OF ONE MILE PER HOUR...

DAD, IS A SHAPE A SPACE?
TALKING ABOUT SPACE: DID YOU CLEAN YOUR ROOM?
IT'S NOT BECAUSE A CLEAN SPACE CONTAINS SOME DIRTY SHAPES THAT IT'S A DIRTY ROOM BY DEFINITION...
THE CONCEPTUAL THINKING PHASE IS STARTING WAY TOO EARLY...
HE'S **YOUR** SON...

WHY DO WE HAVE TO DESIGN EVERYTHING?
CAN'T WE JUST LEAVE THINGS FOR WHAT THEY ARE?
IF WE DON'T DESIGN THEM THEN GOD WILL, AND THAT'S SOMETHING TOTALLY DIFFERENT...
I WISH I HAD LEFT MAN FOR WHAT HE WAS...

I WAS AT A PARTY SITTING NEXT TO AN ARCHITECT AND ALL HE COULD TALK ABOUT WAS HIS ARCHITECTURE... I DIDN'T EVEN GET THE CHANCE TO TALK ABOUT MY ARCHITECTURE...
DON'T GET ME WRONG... I DON'T HAVE ANYTHING AGAINST EGOISM...
BUT IT HAS TO GIVE OTHER EGOISM A CHANCE TOO...
I KNOW...
THERE'S STILL A LOT OF WORK TO BE DONE WHEN IT COMES TO SELFISHNESS...

WHY ARE YOU ALWAYS WHINING ABOUT DETAILS? YOU'D BETTER FOCUS ON THE BIGGER PICTURE!
WACK
SOMETIMES CONTRACTORS ARE RIGHT...
WHO'S GOING TO BUILD OUR PROJECT NOW?
MINOR DETAIL...

ARCHIBALD HAS LANDED A NEW PROJECT... HE'S WORKING ON IT AT FULL SPEED...
POP
WHAT WAS THAT?!
MY EGO BROKE THROUGH THE SOUND BARRIER...

READY?
EHH...
PUT ME DOWN!
PUT ME DOWN!
~~SKYSCRAPER~~

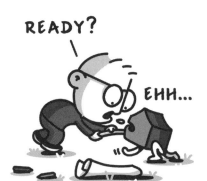

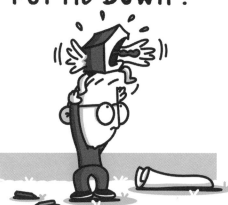

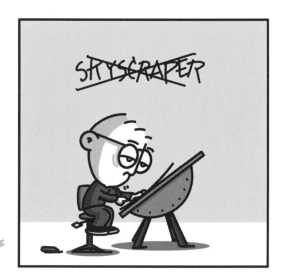

ARCHITECTURE ! ARCHITECTURE ! ARCHITECTURE !
AND NOW LIKE IF YOU REALLY MEAN IT !
WHAT ARE YOU ?
ARCHITECTURE !
ARCHITECTURE ! ARCHITECTURE ! ARCHITECTURE !
YOU'RE TAKING BUILDING IDENTITY WAY TOO SERIOUSLY...
IT'S NOT BECAUSE IT'S A DESIGN FOR A BAR THAT A FAKE ID WILL GET HIM IN...
I'M A STRIP CLUB !

AT SCHOOL THEY SAID AS AN ARCHITECT I WOULD MAKE A LOT OF MONEY...
DID THEY ALSO TELL YOU THAT YOUR CHANCES TO GET RICH ARE BIGGER IF YOU'RE POOR AS AN INTERN?
NO...
I CAN MAKE YOU VERY POOR...
REALLY?! ARE YOU WILLING TO DO THAT FOR ME?!
THEY WILL BE RIGHT AT SCHOOL AFTER ALL... WE'RE GONNA BE RICH...

YEEHAAA
SPLAT
DIDN'T I ALREADY EXPLAIN TO YOU THAT THIS TYPE OF CARDBOARD IS TOO SMOOTH?

AAARGH!
I'M BEING EATEN BY MY DESIGN!
IN FIFTEEN YEARS A HARSH REALITY FOR YOU...
HA !
I'LL DESIGN AN EMERGENCY EXIT AT THE BACK !

I'VE SUMMARIZED THE PROJECT IN ONE SINGLE SKETCH...
NO NO... THAT'S IMPOSSIBLE...
THE DESIGN PROCESS IS VERY COMPLEX... YOU NEED VERY SOPHISTICATED BRAINS TO EVEN COMPREHEND IT...
HEY YOU ! DOES THIS GO LEFT OR RIGHT AROUND?

DAD ! TODAY WE WENT ON A SCHOOL TRIP TO THE MUSEUM ! AND GUESS HOW WIDE THE ENTRANCE WAS !
THIS WIDE !
IT'S GOOD YOU CAN USE YOUR ARMS FOR MEASURING...
WHEN I'M ALL GROWN UP I'LL GET TO MEASURE EVEN BETTER !
I'LL HAVE ROOM FOR MORE LINES !

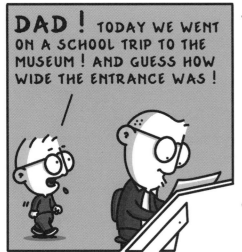

DAD, CAN YOU GIVE ME A HAND WITH THIS SAW, PROSTHETIC ARM AND THESE BOLTS?
WHAT ARE YOU UP TO?!
I USE MY ARMS TO MEASURE AND I WANT TO CREATE A FOLDING MEASURE SO I CAN STRETCH FARTHER...
I HADN'T REALIZED THAT ARCHITECTS MEASURE BY EYE...
WHERE AM I GONNA FIND A GLASS EYE?

DAD, WHO DESIGNS OUR SLEEP?
SLEEP DESIGN IS A SPECIAL COURSE IN ARCHITECTURE SCHOOL...
SO YOU DESIGN IT?
YES AND FOR YOU ALSO...
IT'S BEDTIME
CAN'T YOU DESIGN IT TO BE LATER?
CAN YOU STAY UP LATER?
IT'S A DANGER FOR THE STABI-LITY OF THE DAY

WHAT HAVE YOU DONE TO MY DESIGN?!
I'VE DESIGNED ITS SLEEP...
IT'S ONE BIG BEDROOM?!
IT'S A LIVING ROOM DURING THE DAY...
AT 11 AM ?
HEY !
PROVIDING LIVING SPACE IS A VERY TIRING PURSUIT !
ESPECIALLY TO A SIX YEAR OLD ARCHITECT

I'M A DESIGN...
YOU LOVE DESIGNS...
YOU CAN'T
DESTROY ME !
SWAT
YOU LOOK MUCH
BETTER ON PAPER...

CRUMPLE
CRUMPLE
POC
THANK GOD MY REJECTED
DESIGNS CAN'T EXIST
OUTSIDE THIS SPACE...

SOMETIMES I WONDER IF THIS IS ALL THAT LIFE HAS TO OFFER...
AND THEN I DESIGN THIS !
THIS IS NOT WHAT I WANT !
NO... THIS IS IT...

THE CLIENT IS SUING US FOR BREACH OF CONTRACT...
A DIFFERENCE OF OPINION ON THE COLOR OF A SCREW ISN'T ENOUGH OF A REASON TO STOP THE COLLABORATION...
HE'S THE ONE MAKING A PROBLEM OUT OF IT...
OH...

SO... A PLAN IS A HORIZONTAL SECTION?
RIGHT...
THERE'S ONE THING I DON'T QUITE UNDERSTAND...
HOW DO YOU SLICE A BUILDING THIS THIN?
THE CONTRACTOR ASKS WHERE WE GOT OUR GRINDING DISC...

WHY ARE YOU STARING AT THAT LINE ?!
IF YOU ZOOM IN YOU'LL NOTICE IT'S A BUILDING...
YOU ARE HERE TO DESIGN STRIKING BUILDINGS !
WHAT DO YOU MEAN?
A BUILDING THAT CAN HIDE BEHIND A LINE ISN'T STRIKING ENOUGH!

DID YOU KNOW THAT AN ARCHITECT IS A KIND OF DIRECTOR? AND A SITE A SORT OF SET?
NO...
ACTION !
BUT THE ACTORS DON'T ALWAYS FOLLOW THE SCRIPT...

I ONLY WORK WITH CONTRACTORS WHO ARE TALLER THAN MY SPECS...
AND WHO APPRECIATE IT'S WELL-FOUNDED...
AAAAAA!

YOU STUPID IDIOT OF A CLIENT, I'M NOT ANSWERING ALL YOUR DUMB QUESTIONS ! I HATE YOU ! LEAVE ME ALONE !
send !
are you sure you want to send this ? Y N
are you really sure? Y N
really really sure? Y N
yes! yes! yes!
CLICK CLICK CLICK
this email has been deleted.
THE SAFETY MANAGER IS PUSHING IT...

HAVE YOU EVER CONSIDERED SHAVING BEFORE COMING TO WORK?
FRED, CAN YOU SAND DOWN THE TOP OF THIS FLOOR BOARD FOR ME?
YOU WERE SAYING?
NEVER MIND...
KERR

OH BOY... I'M EXCITED TO MEET THE NEW CLIENT !
WHATEVER YOU DO DON'T RUB YOUR STAIRS IN HIS FACE
SLRRP
I THINK I'LL PASS ON A HOUSE WITH MULTIPLE LEVELS...
WHAT DID I TELL YOU?
BUT HE'S SO CLIMBABLE

REMEMBER ME?
?
YOU USED TO LOVE ME...
SMACK
THE LOVE FOR A FIRST DRAFT IS HEAVILY OVERRATED...

REASONS WHY I HATE BEING AN ARCHITECT:
1.CLIENTS WITHOUT VISION
2.INCOMPETENT CONTRACTORS
3.GOVERNMENT REGULATIONS
TELL ME AGAIN: WHY DO I LOVE ARCHITECTURE?
THE MONEY?
DO I HAVE A REASON WITH AN EXPIRATION DATE LONGER THAN FIFTEEN SECONDS?

THE CLIENT IS HERE FOR THE MEETING ! YOU COMING?
I DON'T THINK SO... I HATE THAT GUY...
ZOOF
THERE'S CAKE IN THE SHAPE OF THE CLIENT !
OUCH ! HE BIT MY NOSE !
MISTAKES HAPPEN IN ARCHITECTURE...

CHECK IT OUT !
I HAVE CREATED THE BEST DESIGN IN THE WORLD...
OK...
ARCHITECTURE IS NOT ABOUT "HAVING" BUT ABOUT "BEING"...
I AM THE BEST ARCHITECT IN THE WORLD....
HE PUTS THE "I" IN ARCHITECTURE...

I WISH I COULD RAISE MY CLIENTS LIKE THEY WERE MY OWN CHILDREN !
IT'S A WASTE OF TIME AND MONEY
BY THE TIME THEY'RE EIGHTEEN THEY PROBABLY MARRY SOMEONE RAISED BY CLIENTS AND THEN YOU'RE SCREWED ANYWAY...
NOT IF I DO MY BEST AS A PARENT
DAD, MY GIRLFRIEND DOESN'T LIKE YOUR ARCHITECTURE...
I REST MY CASE...

THE CITY IS FULL...
NEW BUILDINGS CAN ONLY BE ADDED AFTER ANOTHER ONE IS DEMOLISHED...
urban development department
HERE'S MY DESIGN PROPOSAL...
TICK
TOCK
TICK
TOCK
urban development department
THEY CHANGED THEIR POLICY...

SOMETIMES I WISH I WASN'T AN ARCHITECT...

WHY IS THAT?

THEN I WOULD STOP SEEING EVERYTHING IN TERMS OF CONSTRUCTION...

YOU MISSED THE CLIENT'S DEADLINE !
IS THAT A BAD THING?
NOW WE HAVE TO PAY A FINE...
YOU CAN TAKE IT OFF MY PAY
YOU ALREADY OWE FIVE LIFETIMES OF PAY...
YOU MISSED A DEADLINE...

ALL THAT THINKING...
SOMETIMES I WISH I COULD
DO SOMETHING PHYSICAL...
DRAW DRAW DRAW DRAW
DRAW DRAW DRAW DRAW
DRAW DRAW DRAW DRAW
DRAW DRAW DRAW DRAW
THAT FELT GOOD...
AHH...

THANK YOU ALL FOR ATTENDING THIS MEETING...
SORRY, THE CLIENT IS LATE...
TOO LATE ! EVERYONE HAS ALREADY APPROVED MY DESIGN !
NICE REHEARSAL...
IN REALITY IT'S HARDER TO HIDE THE CLIENT...

PFFF… I RUSH FROM ONE CONSTRUCTION DELAY TO ANOTHER…
I NEED A CUP OF COFFEE…
THE COFFEE CONTRACTOR HAS SOME DELAY…

I HEARD YOU REFUSE TO USE THE MATERIALS THAT I PRESCRIBED...
YOU MAKE IT SOUND LIKE IT'S SOME SORT OF MEDICATION TO CURE ME...
NO... IT'S TO CURE THE BUILDING FROM YOU!
THE DISEASE IS SPREADING MORE WIDELY THAN WE ANTICIPATED...

GOD, WHY DIDN'T YOU DESIGN A PLANET THAT IS IMPOSSIBLE TO POLLUTE ? IT WOULD HAVE SAVED ME A LOT OF TROUBLE DESIGNING SUSTAINABLE ARCHITECTURE...
I DID... BUT DESIGNING IS ALSO ABOUT LEAVING ROOM FOR THE UNEXPECTED...
WHACK
I DIDN'T SEE THAT ONE COMING...
THAT'S BECAUSE I'M A GREAT DESIGNER...

IT'S BETTER TO HAVE A GOOD CUP OF COFFEE IN AN UGLY ENVIRONMENT THAN A BAD ONE IN A NICE ENVIRONMENT...
WHY IS THAT?
GOOD COFFEE MAKES THE ENVIRONMENT NICER...
WELL... THIS IS GREAT COFFEE BUT THE ROOM STILL LOOKS UGLY TO ME...
I WAS TALKING ABOUT THE ROOM IN MY HEAD...

MAY I PROUDLY PRESENT YOUR PROJECT !
THE DESIGN ISN'T FINISHED YET...
LET THE DESIGN SPEAK FOR ITSELF...
I HATE BEING A HOUSE... I WANT TO HAVE A FUNCTION CHANGE OPERATION
I ALREADY HAVE HIS LINEAR ELEMENTS REMOVED...

WHAT'S WITH THE EXTRA MODEL?
HEY
PSST
SOME CLIENTS HAVE SPECIFIC NEEDS WHEN IT COMES TO THE PRESENTATION OF THE INTERIOR...

HE'S SO CAUGHT UP IN HIS DESIGN AGAIN THAT HE DOESN'T KNOW HE'S HOME
HONEY, I'M GONNA BE HOME LATE AGAIN !
OK... CAN YOU STOP BY THE STORE ON YOUR WAY HOME?
MY IMAGINATION TAKES ME AWAY FROM HOME FOR THE WRONG REASONS...
STORE

HEY DAD ! LOOK ! I DESIGNED A NEW CLIENT !
UNFORTUNATELY YOU CAN'T DESIGN REAL PEOPLE...
I ALREADY SUSPECTED ARCHITECTS WEREN'T REAL PEOPLE...
WHY DO YOU SAY THAT?
BECAUSE THEY DESIGNED THEMSELVES: BLACK SUIT, WHITE SHIRT AND BLACK ROUND GLASSES...

WHAT ARE YOU DOING? CAN'T YOU SEE THE WORLD HAS TOO MANY BUILDINGS?
DON'T WORRY, GOD...
I HAVE THE PERFECT SOLUTION... WE CONTINUE TO BUILD UNTIL ALL INDIVIDUAL BUILDINGS FORM BUT ONE SINGLE BUILDING...
AND WHAT ARE YOU GOING TO DO ABOUT THE FACT THAT THERE ARE TOO MANY PEOPLE?
I GOT THAT COVERED TOO
I ALREADY FEEL LIKE THREE HUNDRED ARCHITECTS TOGETHER

WHAT'S THAT ON YOUR FACE?
WHILE SHAVING I HAD AN IDEA FOR A DESIGN ...
I NEVER IMAGINED I WOULD KISS A BUSHY BUILDING...
IF I USE MY TONGUE I CAN ENLARGE THE WINDOWS...
SO MUCH FOR MY ROMANTIC MORNING KISS...
HEY ! IT'S A NICE COZY ENGLISH COTTAGE !

YOU'RE READY ! LET'S GO OUTSIDE AND PLAY !
I'D RATHER STAY INSIDE...
WHAT? I'VE NEVER HEARD OF A BUILDING STAYING INSIDE...
AN EXTRA FAÇADE MEANS BETTER INSULATION...
75
TODAY'S BUILDINGS ARE SISSIES...

SO YOU DON'T FEEL LIKE GOING OUTSIDE?
NO...
MAYBE IT'S BECAUSE YOU'RE NOT READY YET?
YES... LIKE I'M NOT EVEN BORN YET...
OF COURSE... THAT'S IT ! OUR HOUSE IS PREGNANT !
DAD... I'VE ALWAYS WONDERED WHY YOU DESIGNED OUR HOUSE SO BIG AND FAT BUT NOW I KNOW...

THIS BUILDING IS WAY TOO EXPRESSIVE... IT INSULTS THE ENVIRONMENT...
ONLY FROM TIME TO TIME...
BUILDING PERMITS
PAINTED GLASS ! UNTREATED WOOD ! PRINTED CONCRETE !
BUILDING PERMITS
DESIGN TOURETTE SYNDROME IS STILL TABOO...

WHAT'S THIS?
I'M OPENING A BAR TO TAKE OUT THE COMPETITION...
HOW ARE YOU GOING TO DO THAT?
I MAKE THEM DRUNK SO THEIR DESIGNS WILL GET ALL MESSED UP...
IS IT WORKING?
ONLY WITH SOME OF THEM...
MORNING MR. GEHRY... THE USUAL?
YES...TWENTY-THREE SHOTS OF WHISKEY

DAD... I DREAMED THAT I WAS A BUILDING AND THAT MY SEWERAGE WAS LEAKING...
BUT DON'T WORRY... I ALREADY FIXED IT !

AH... A SANDWICH !
WHAT'S ON IT?
ARCHITECT'S TONGUE...
MAKES HIM SHUT UP EVERY TIME...

THIS IS JUNK !
GO BACK TO THE DRAWING BOARD !
WACK
THE SOUL OF MY DESIGN...
WHAT'S THAT?
HE'S WAITING TO REINCARNATE INTO THE NEXT DESIGN I'LL MAKE FOR YOU...

DAD, IS WORKING LIKE GOING TO SCHOOL?
IF YOU'RE A DESIGNER, THE SECRET DRAWINGS YOU MAKE IN YOUR SCHOOL BOOKS BECOME REALITY...
WE HAVE TO RUN! THE TEACHER'S MUTANTS ARE COMING!

WHERE'S MY MODEL?!
ARCHIE ! HOW MANY TIMES DO I HAVE TO TELL YOU !
STOP PLAYING WITH MY MODELS!
THEN STOP MAKING THEM ON A KID SCALE...
YEAH ! MAKE ME AN ADULT BUILDING!

WHEN I BECOME AN ARCHITECT I'M GONNA MAKE THE WORLD A BETTER PLACE...
WHAT ARE YOU GOING TO DO IN THE MEANTIME?
LETTING EVERYONE KNOW THAT THIS IS NOT A GOOD PLACE...
THIS BUILDING SUCKS!
PSSSS
IF YOU CONTINUE THIS UNTIL YOU GRADUATE, YOUR JOB WILL BE A LOT EASIER...
THAT'S WHY I AM A VISIONARY ARCHITECT...

YOU LOOK PRETTY BUSY...
I'VE GOT TEN CLIENT MEETINGS TODAY...
I DIDN'T KNOW YOU HAVE THAT MANY PROJECTS GOING ON...
I DON'T...
BUT IF I TREAT EVERY CLIENT REMARK AS A MEETING, I CAN CANCEL A FEW...

ARCHIE, WHAT ARE YOU DOING?
REDESIGNING THE SCHOOL !
THAT WAS NOT THE ASSIGNMENT !
GO TO THE PRINCIPAL'S OFFICE !
ACCORDING TO MY PLAN IT MUST BE RIGHT HERE...
HE'S NOT IN HIS OFFICE... HIS SEAT IS DOWN...

ARCHIE ! ANSWER THE QUESTION !
I CAN'T... I FEEL SPATIALLY OPPRESSED! "THIRTY KIDS" MAKES THIS ROOM TOO SMALL!
AND BEFORE YOU SAY ANYTHING: DETENTION MAKES IT TOO LARGE...
THERE'S NO SPATIAL BALANCE IN THIS SCHOOL...

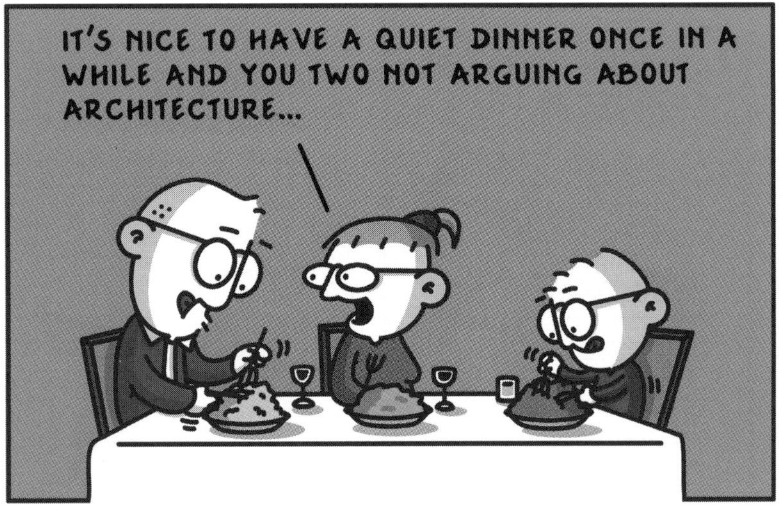
IT'S NICE TO HAVE A QUIET DINNER ONCE IN A WHILE AND YOU TWO NOT ARGUING ABOUT ARCHITECTURE...

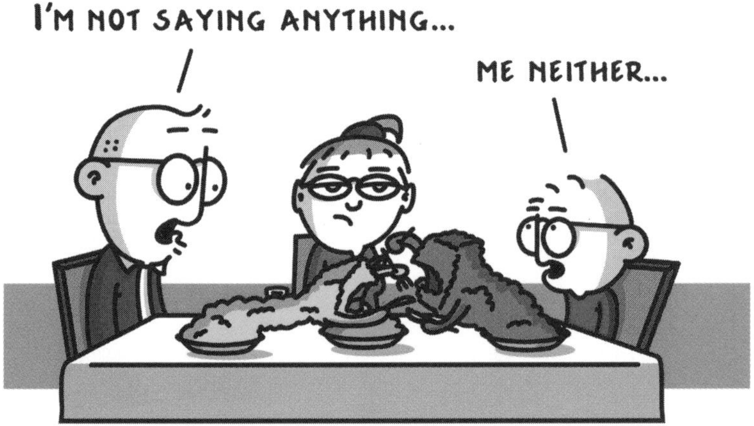
I'M NOT SAYING ANYTHING...
ME NEITHER...

TSACK!
AAA
A NORTH ARROW? REALLY?
I THINK IT'S MORE PLEASANT HAVING THE SUN SNEAK UP ON THE BACK OF A HOUSE...

GREAT ! YOU'VE CLEANED UP YOUR ROOM...
I HIRED A CONTRACTOR TO DO THE JOB !
HERE'S THE BILL...
I DON'T GET IT... HE DOES THE SAME...
WHAT'S THE DIFFERENCE BETWEEN BUILDING AND CLEANING UP AN ENVIRONMENT?

ONCE UPON A TIME THERE WAS AN ARCHITECT WHO WANTED TO MAKE THE WORLD A BETTER PLACE...
VERY NICE DAD, BUT NOW I'M WIDE AWAKE !
NOW I FEEL LIKE DESIGNING...

WHAT ARE YOU DOING?!!! YOU SHOULD BE DEFENDING THIS SPACE!
PEOPLE ARE HAPPIER WHEN THIS SPACE IS FILLED...
I DON'T GET SOCCER ARCHITECTURE...
POC

AAA
ACHOO
I ALWAYS START WITH THE LANDSCAPE...

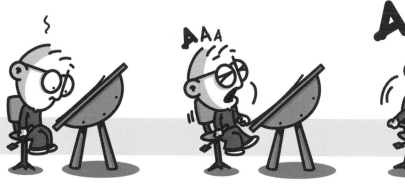

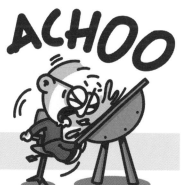

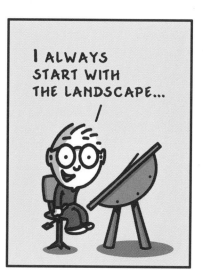

Mike Hermans, pseudonym "Maaik" (born Antwerp, March 25, 1971) is himself an architect. Raised in Antwerp, Maaik studied architecture at the University of Antwerp. To visualize his ideas, Maaik used his own figures to determine human proportions, which soon evolved into comic figures. A cartoonist was born. Some added dialogue was enough to create the humorous world of Archibald. Maaik devised Archibald from real life experiences. He is the reflection of Maaik's own views on architecture. Maaik recognized a way to exercise the profession of architect as he always wanted: with a sense of humor. Archibald is the would-be architect in him and the only architect he ever wants to be… Architecture is shaping the space within himself…

STOP IT! THERE'S NOTHING FUNNY ABOUT ARCHITECTURE!

MIKE HERMANS   ARCHIBALD

The *Deutsche Bibliothek* lists this publication in the *Deutsche National-bibliografie*; detailed bibliographic data is available on the internet at http://dnb.d-nb.de

ISBN 978-3-86922-440-4

A DOM publishers

© 2015 by DOM publishers, Berlin
www.dom-publishers.com

Proofreading
Virginia Tanzmann

Printing
Print House Dimiter Blagoev, Sofia

FOLLOW THE LIFE OF ARCHIBALD ON
WWW.ARCHMAAIK.COM

with special thanks to:
Virginia Tanzmann for editing the
strips and texts in this book and her
advice on architecture life... Philipp
and Natascha Meuser for publishing
this book and their support with
the strip... My wife Eva Koninckx.
Archibald wouldn't exist without her...